Mommy's Here:
A Guided Journal for New Moms

Written by:
Sharifa Brown

Disclaimer:
This book contains the thoughts, opinions, and prompts by the author. The author is not your healthcare professional. Please understand that the suggestions in this book are not intended as a substitute for the medical advice from trained health professionals. Be sure to follow the recommendations from your physician or healthcare professionals regarding suggestions or recommendation(s) that are provided in this book. The author and publisher do not assume any responsibility and hereby disclaim any liability in terms of damage, loss, or risk by the utilization and implementation of any of the content provided in this book.

Copyright © 2021 by Sharifa Brown

All Rights Reserved. No part of this publication may be reproduced or transmitted in any form without written permission of the author and publisher.

ISBN 978-1-7361846-5-3

Written by: Sharifa Brown

Cover design and Illustration by: Maria Charina Gomez

Congratulations Mama!

This journal belongs to an AMAZINGLY STRONG MAMA named

_____

On, _____/_____/_____
         Month   Date   Year

a beautiful baby was born named

_____

Weight: _____

Length: _____

Time: _____

Hospital: _____

Parents: _____
_____

Place Your Photo Here

♥Visitors♥

Date	Name

♥Visitors♥

Date	Name

♥ How are you doing, Mama? ♥

♥ How are you doing, Mama? ♥

❤ How are you doing, Mama? ❤

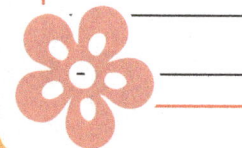

♥ How are you doing, Mama? ♥

Color Me

Go Ahead and draw the PLUS sign!

When you realized you were pregnant, what was the first emotion you experienced?

What was your partner's reaction to your pregnancy?

After you told your partner, who was the next person you told about your pregnancy? How did they react?

How are you doing, Mama?

♥ How are you doing, Mama? ♥

How are you doing, Mama?

♥ How are you doing, Mama? ♥

Did you have any weird dreams during your pregnancy?

What was the best thing about being pregnant?

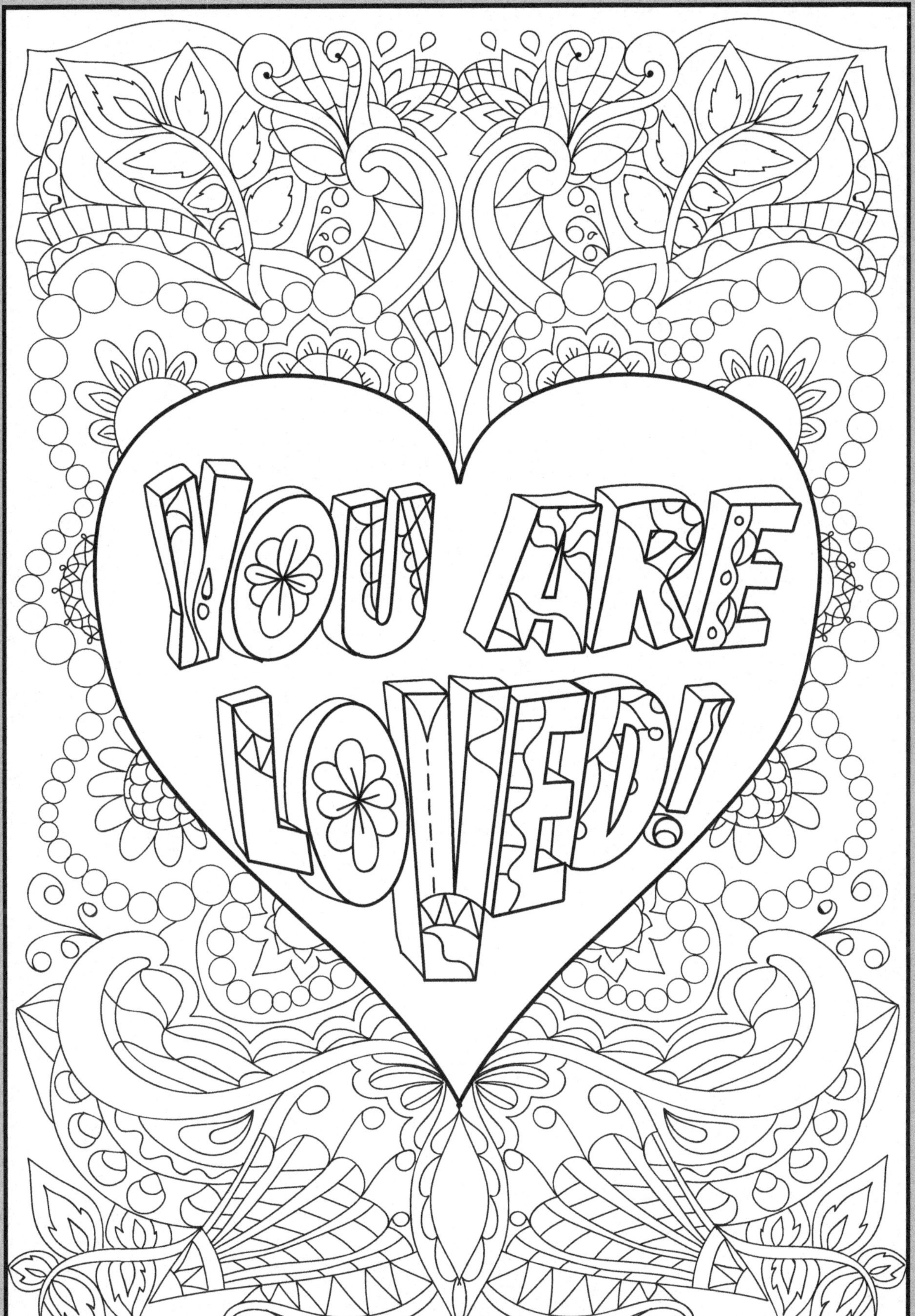
YOU ARE
LOVED!

Name some of foods you craved during your pregnancy.

How did you choose your baby's name?

Name 5 personality traits you would like to pass down your child:

♥ How are you doing, Mama? ♥

♥ How are you doing, Mama? ♥

♥ How are you doing, Mama? ♥

♥ How are you doing, Mama? ♥

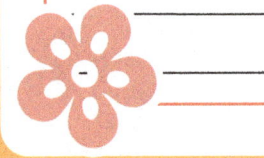

What was the first emotion you experienced when you realized you were in labor? Journal your labor experience.

What came to your mind the moment you laid eyes on your little one?

Mother's Milk

How did you feel when you held your baby for the first time?

What was your partner's reaction to your pregnancy?

Take a moment to mute all the sounds around you: phone, television, etc. Ask those around you to give you a few moments of solitude and silence. Cuddle your child; hold their hand. At this moment, it's just you and your little one. Focus on your baby's scent and the feeling of their skin. Now, write down your feelings below:

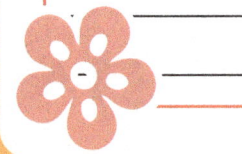

♥ How are you doing, Mama? ♥

♥ How are you doing, Mama? ♥

♥ How are you doing, Mama? ♥

How are you doing, Mama?

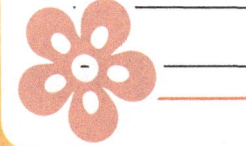

You are doing Awesome!

What is your favorite song to sing to your baby?
Why did you choose this song?

**Write down a song that makes you feel happy?
Why did you pick this song?**

Read to your baby

What is your favorite book to read to your baby? Why?

♥ How are you doing, Mama? ♥

How are you doing, Mama?

♥ How are you doing, Mama? ♥

♥ How are you doing, Mama? ♥

Don't be afraid to speak up! You are your baby's advocate.
Ask as many questions as you need regarding you little's one care.
Write some of your questions on this page.

Develop your own personal opinions. Listen to advice, but follow you own heart. This is YOUR baby! Write down some advice that you've received. Do you agree or disagree?

Trust Your Instincts

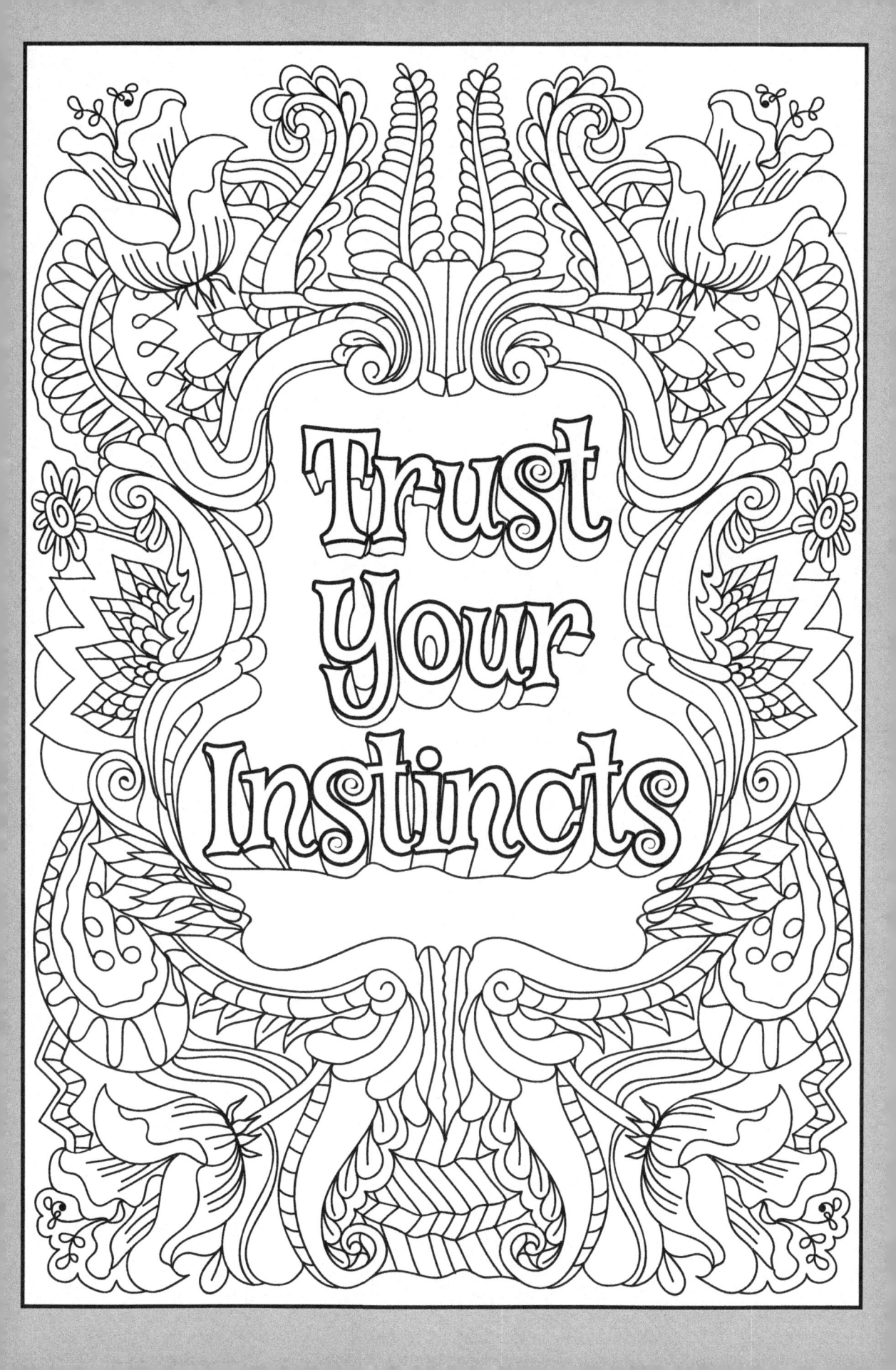

Write down 5 negative thoughts, then, using a red marker, draw a giant X on each one of them!

♥ How are you doing, Mama? ♥

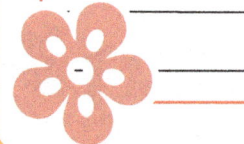

♥ How are you doing, Mama? ♥

♥ How are you doing, Mama? ♥

♥ How are you doing, Mama? ♥

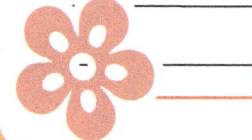

The Journey will be tough,
but let's find a way to get through this!

SOLUTION

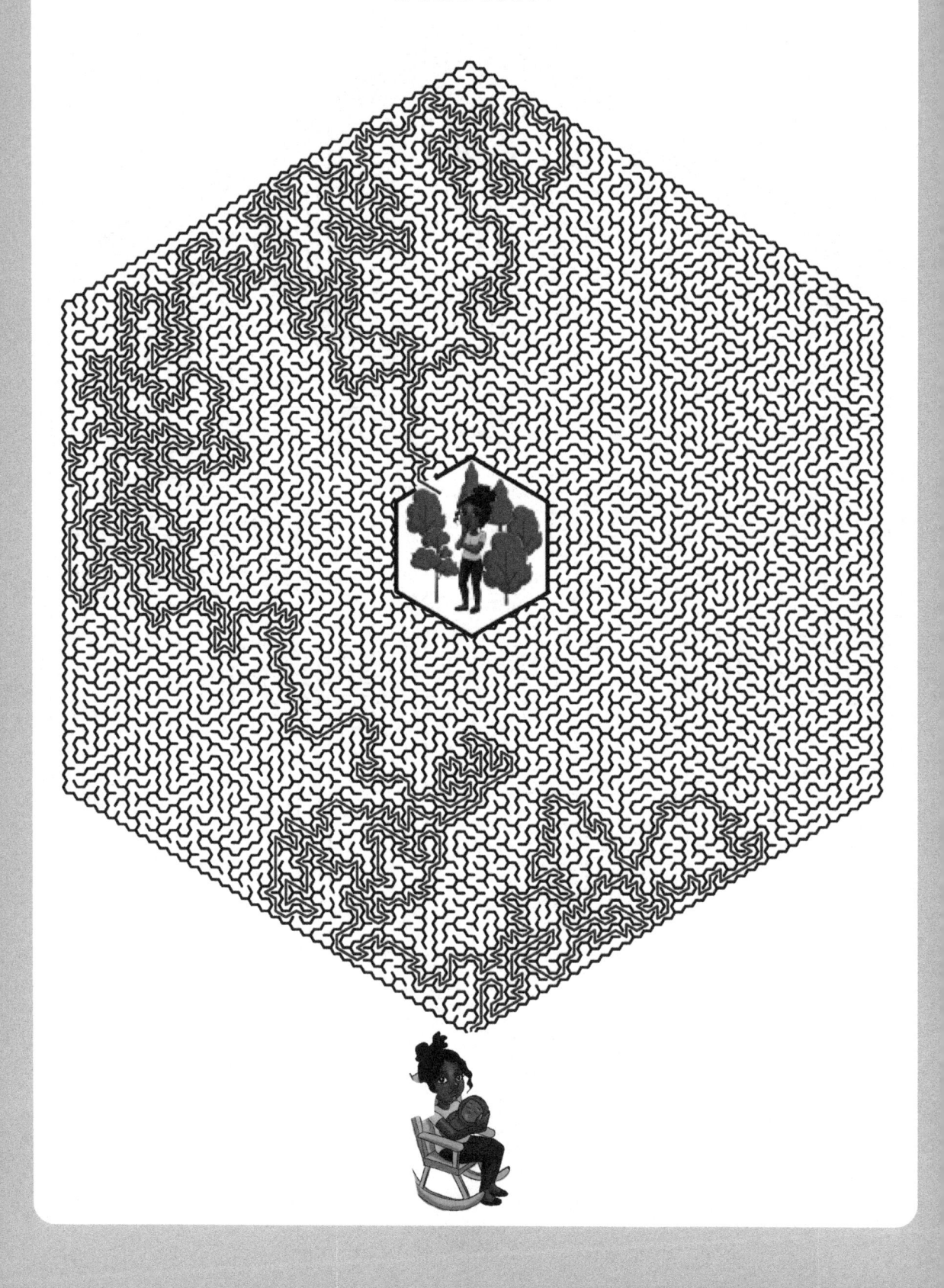

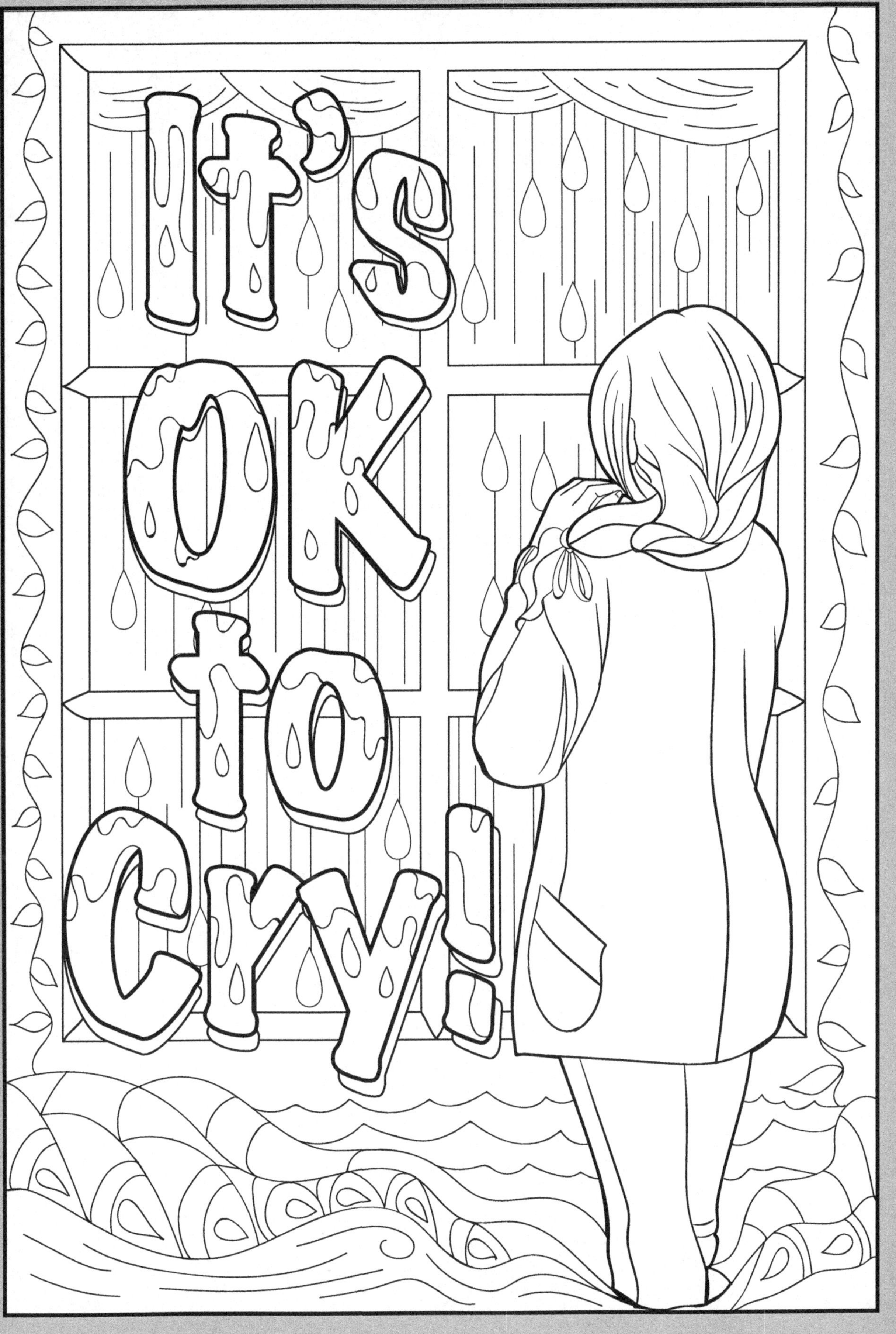
It's OK to Cry!

It's ok to CRY! Let those feelings out, Mama! Write down your feelings.

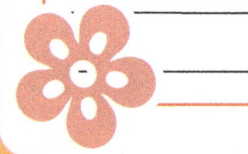

♥ How are you doing, Mama? ♥

♥ How are you doing, Mama? ♥

♥ How are you doing, Mama? ♥

♥ How are you doing, Mama? ♥

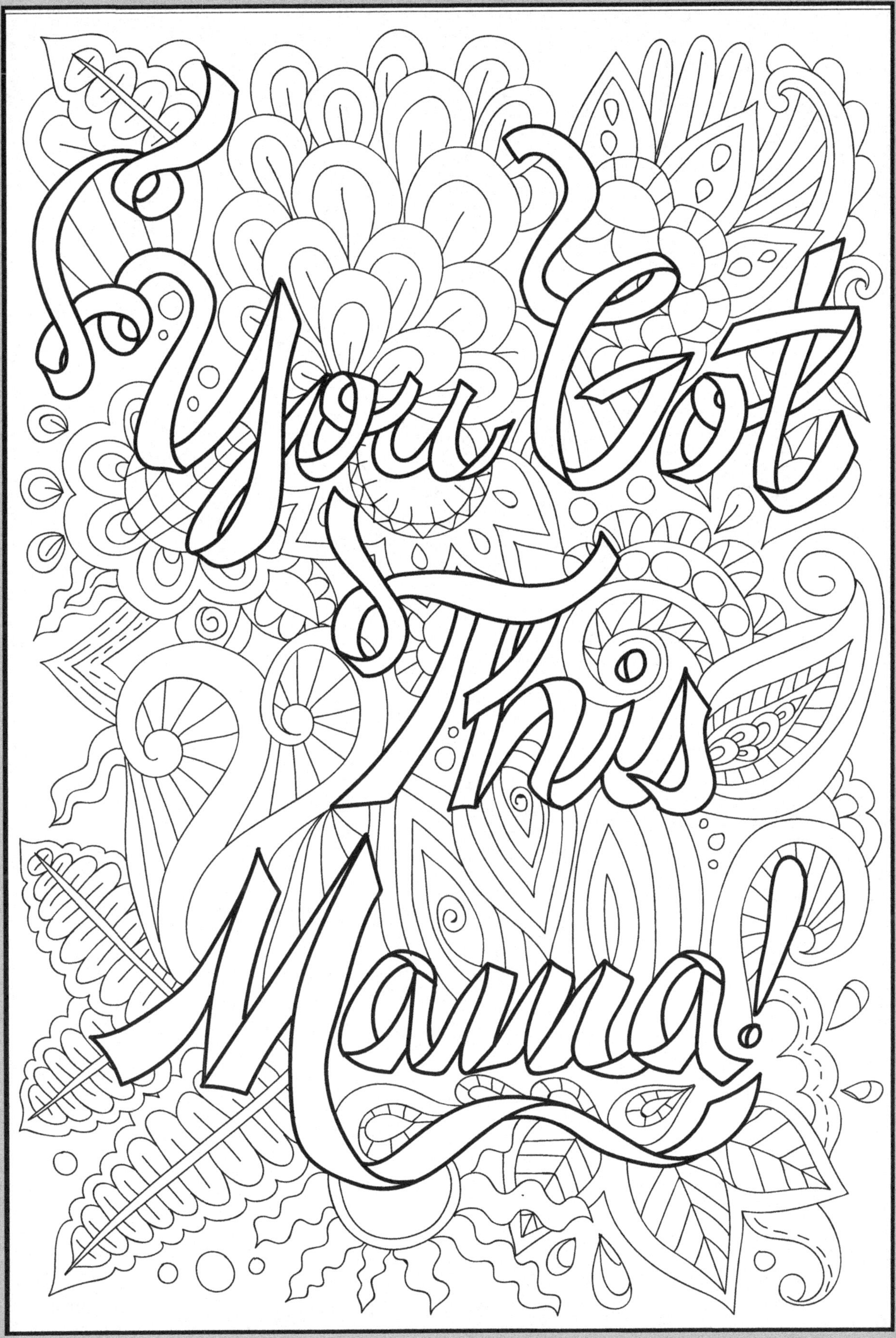
You Got
This
Mama!

Write down some terrible or negative advice or statements someone told you. Now immediately erase those words from this page as well as your mind! No room for negativity!

Write down all the fears or worries in your mind. Now throw those fears away!

It takes time to heal.
Fill in the bandages with things that make you feel better.

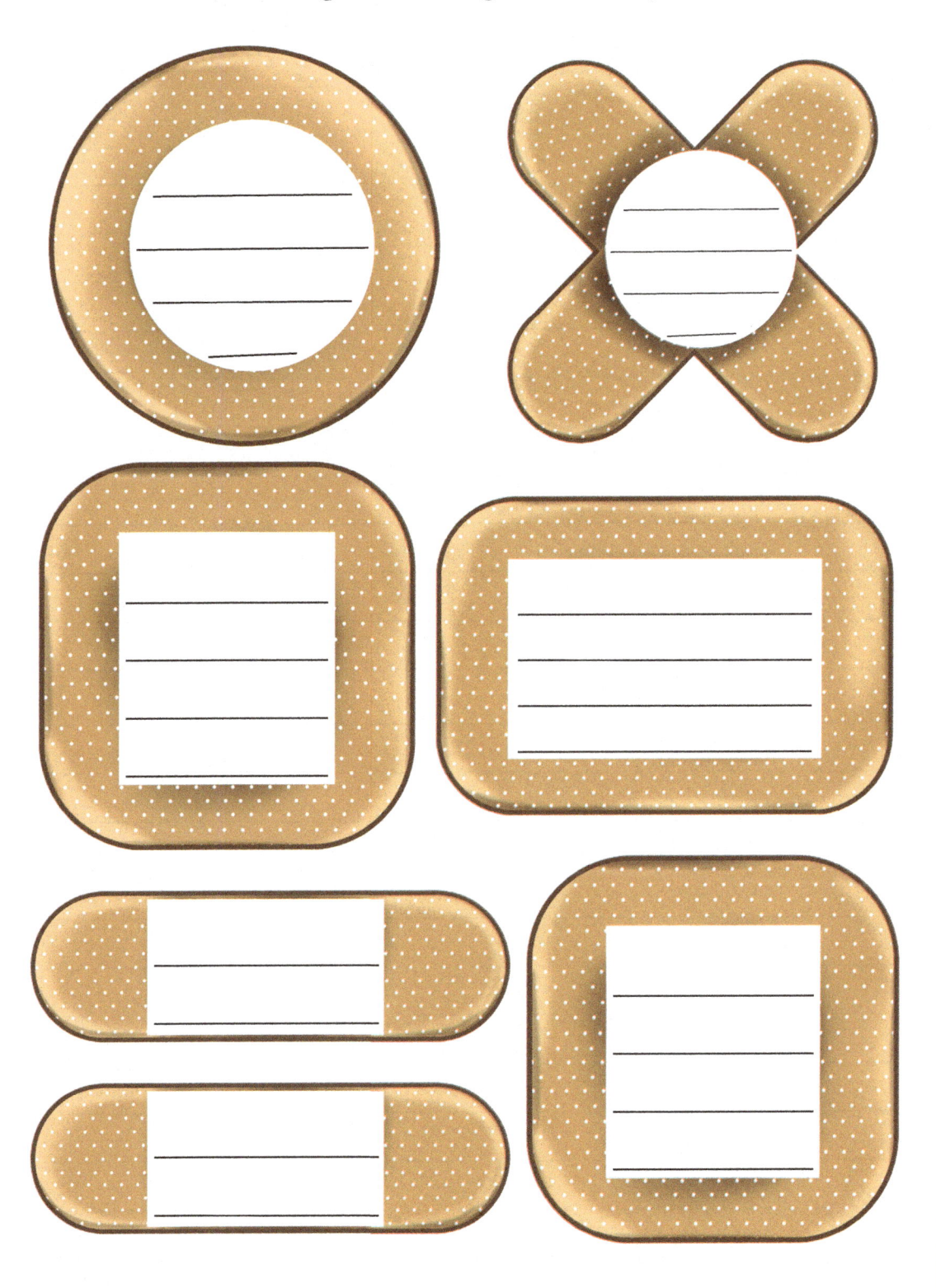

♥ How are you doing, Mama? ♥

How are you doing, Mama?

♥ How are you doing, Mama? ♥

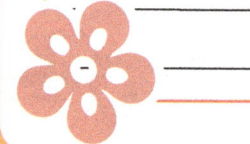

♥ How are you doing, Mama? ♥

Don't be puzzled. Try this instead!

Puzzle 1

7		1		8	3	9		
	5		2				1	
	3							
4	1	6	9					
		3	8		7	1		
					2	4	3	5
							4	
	8				9		7	
		4	5	1		2		3

Puzzle 2

	4	7	6	1	3		2	
8						9	7	
2			7					
3			9					
	9		5		4		8	
					1			9
					6			4
	8	2						7
	1		8	9	7	6	3	

SOLUTIONS

Puzzle 1

7	4	1	6	8	3	9	5	2
6	5	8	2	9	4	3	1	7
2	3	9	7	5	1	8	6	4
4	1	6	9	3	5	7	2	8
5	2	3	8	4	7	1	9	6
8	9	7	1	6	2	4	3	5
1	6	2	3	7	8	5	4	9
3	8	5	4	2	9	6	7	1
9	7	4	5	1	6	2	8	3

Puzzle 2

9	4	7	6	1	3	5	2	8
8	6	3	4	5	2	9	7	1
2	5	1	7	8	9	3	4	6
3	2	4	9	6	8	7	1	5
1	9	6	5	7	4	2	8	3
5	7	8	2	3	1	4	6	9
7	3	9	1	2	6	8	5	4
6	8	2	3	4	5	1	9	7
4	1	5	8	9	7	6	3	2

Don't be puzzled. Try this instead!

Puzzle 3

		7	6					
9	3			8			2	
5	4			7	9	3	1	6
								1
	6			5			7	
4								
6	8	2	9	1			4	3
	9			6			5	8
					4	1		

Puzzle 4

			2				3	
	8	3	5	6				
				9			7	
		9		7			6	1
4	1	6				7	8	3
7	3			8		9		
	5			3				
				5	6	3	2	
	4			2				

SOLUTIONS

Puzzle 3

2	1	7	6	4	3	8	9	5
9	3	6	5	8	1	4	2	7
5	4	8	2	7	9	3	1	6
7	2	9	4	3	6	5	8	1
8	6	3	1	5	2	9	7	4
4	5	1	7	9	8	6	3	2
6	8	2	9	1	5	7	4	3
1	9	4	3	6	7	2	5	8
3	7	5	8	2	4	1	6	9

Puzzle 4

5	9	7	2	4	8	1	3	6
1	8	3	5	6	7	2	9	4
2	6	4	1	9	3	8	7	5
8	2	9	3	7	4	5	6	1
4	1	6	9	2	5	7	8	3
7	3	5	6	8	1	9	4	2
6	5	2	8	3	9	4	1	7
9	7	1	4	5	6	3	2	8
3	4	8	7	1	2	6	5	9

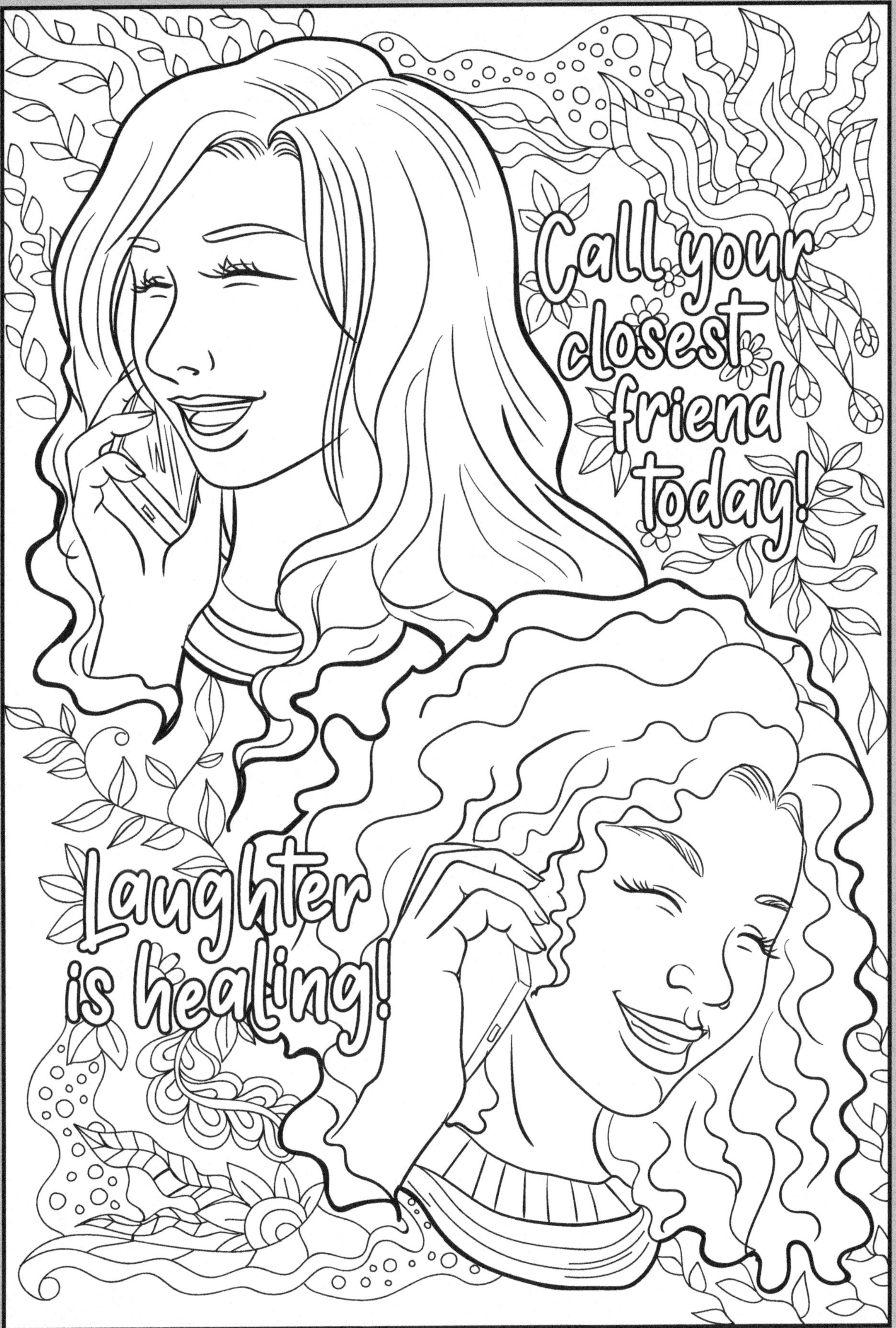
Call your closest friend today!
Laughter is healing!

Ask someone to watch the baby. Go outside, Mom. Feel the sun and wind across your face. Scream as loud as you can and take some deep breaths! Enjoy the healing properties of nature.
Journal your experience.

♥ How are you doing, Mama? ♥

♥ How are you doing, Mama? ♥

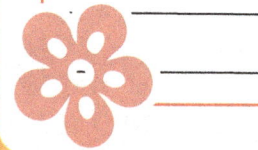

♥ How are you doing, Mama? ♥

♥ How are you doing, Mama? ♥

REWARD ALL VICTORIES, BIG OR SMALL!

WRITE DOWN 3 ACCOMPLISHMENTS!

Sometimes it's hard to find the right words to say!
Find all the positive words you can!

1. Hopeful
2. Optimistic
3. Flourishing
4. Unwavering
5. Exceed
6. Successful
7. Triumphant
8. Miraculous
9. Encouraging
10. Uplifting
11. Motivational
12. Victorious
13. Believe
14. Joyful
15. Grateful
16. Patience
17. Serenity
18. Powerful
19. Capable
20. Fearless
21. Empowered
22. Imaginative
23. Valuable

```
G J B X S U O I R O T C I V N W F L
P X M N P L G W T N A H P M U I R T
E C N E I T A P N E L B A U L A V X
L N Q C X V M O T I V A T I O N A L
G B T T L N V K D X X G D H C E W V
N P D K F H Q B R B N K K T Y X C K
I K Q M F L O U R I S H I N G C M G
G S K U T C N W T R C M V D K E I E
A N U Y N N K F N I G X L M F E M M
R C M O N W I K T T D Z U Y J D A P
U M X D L L A S M M L S F T H L G O
O L W X P U I V G J U L E I Z P I W
C R U U B M C R E C T L P N V G N E
N Z K F I E A A C R B C O E J T A R
E H N T R T L E R A I M H R O G T E
K G P T E E S I P I T N Z E Y N I D
N O M F X S W A E B M X G S F J V R
V C U F F H C O B V G K L K U C E T
L L C U N M T X P B E K N Q L M H X
K Q L V L R C H R Z F E A R L E S S
```

SOLUTION

Sometimes it's hard to find the right words to say!
Find all the positive words you can!

```
G J B X S U O I R O T C I V N W F L
P X M N P L G W T N A H P M U I R T
E C N E I T A P N E L B A U L A V X
L N Q C X V M O T I V A T I O N A L
G B T T L N V K D X X G D H C E W V
N P D K F H Q B R B N K K T Y X C K
I K Q M F L O U R I S H I N G C M G
G S K U T C N W T R C M V D K E I E
A N U Y N N K F N I G X L M F E M M
R C M O N W I K T T D Z U Y J D A P
U M X D L L A S M M L S F T H L G O
O L W X P U I V G J U L E I Z P I W
C R U U B M C R E C T L P N V G N E
N Z K F I E A A C R B C O E J T A R
E H N T R T L E R A I M H R O G T E
K G P T E E S I P I T N Z E Y N I D
N O M F X S W A E B M X G S F J V R
V C U F F H C O B V G K L K U C E T
L L C U N M T X P B E K N Q L M H X
K Q L V L R C H R Z F E A R L E S S
```

Write 3 positive affirmations on the cards.

Let's put them in storage. Come back to this page when you need encouragement.

1.

2.

3.

♥ How are you doing, Mama? ♥

♥ How are you doing, Mama? ♥

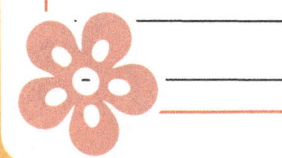

♥ How are you doing, Mama? ♥

♥ How are you doing, Mama? ♥

SMILE MAMA!
Name 3 things that your baby did that made you smile today!

There are so many words to describe your baby!
Let's find some below.

1. Beautiful
2. Miracle
3. Tiny
4. Determined
5. Strength
6. Resilient
7. Courageous
8. Fighter
9. Precious
10. Strong-willed
11. Perseverance
12. Hopeful
13. Loved
14. Innocent
15. Adorable
16. Alert
17. Amazing
18. Sensitive
19. Survivor
20. Fierce
21. Tenacious
22. Worthy
23. Unique

```
R B T D W P M S U R V I V O R F E R
R R M N T R E L A R P R R B N L B F
T V W X Q Q N K Z X E T T L C X P P
C R Z G X N M K T S T D L A B L M T
L H O P E F U L I M E L R O F M B X
R G L J L K Y L J L P I L E V L L L
M R W F T K I Q L T M T U C V E V L
D Z V R Y E T I N Y W E F N Y Z D F
E U Q I N U W V E V A N I A L J Q F
L T D T T G T V T D L A T R S N K R
B H G E N W I T O K D C U E U L Y P
N H G O T T C R Y T T I A V O T R J
N W R N I E A P E M K O E E I S I Q
F T M S I B R N J T R U B S C T N R
S I N W L Z W M B T H S G R E R N Q
B E E E N O A B I R Z G L E R E O Z
S T J R R G J M P N Z C I P P N C F
M N M T C R T B A L E X G F X G E T
X G H T Z E G V K X R D Z K D T N Z
L Y S U O E G A R U O C T M R H T L
```

SOLUTION

There are so many words to describe your baby!
Let's find some below.

Sweet Kisses

Babies need love. How are you showing love to your little one?

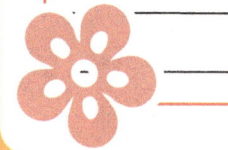

♥ How are you doing, Mama? ♥

♥ How are you doing, Mama? ♥

♥ How are you doing, Mama? ♥

♥ How are you doing, Mama? ♥

Eat Well, Mama!

Nutrition is important!

Your mind can get cluttered sometimes!

Let's find your way back!

SOLUTION

Your mind can get cluttered sometimes!

Let's find your way back!

STOP and REST Mama!

Your body is amazing! What are you doing to take care of yourself, Mama? Write down self-care activities for the upcoming days.

♥ How are you doing, Mama? ♥

♥ How are you doing, Mama? ♥

♥ How are you doing, Mama? ♥

♥ How are you doing, Mama? ♥

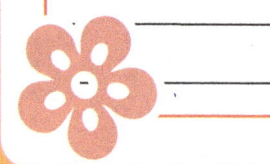

Accept help; it's impossible to do everything on your own.

You don't have to be alone.
Find your support system.

SOLUTION

Write down some helpful advice to another new mom! Make sure to share the advice with her.

How are you doing, Mama?

♥ How are you doing, Mama? ♥

How are you doing, Mama?

♥ How are you doing, Mama? ♥

You are not alone!

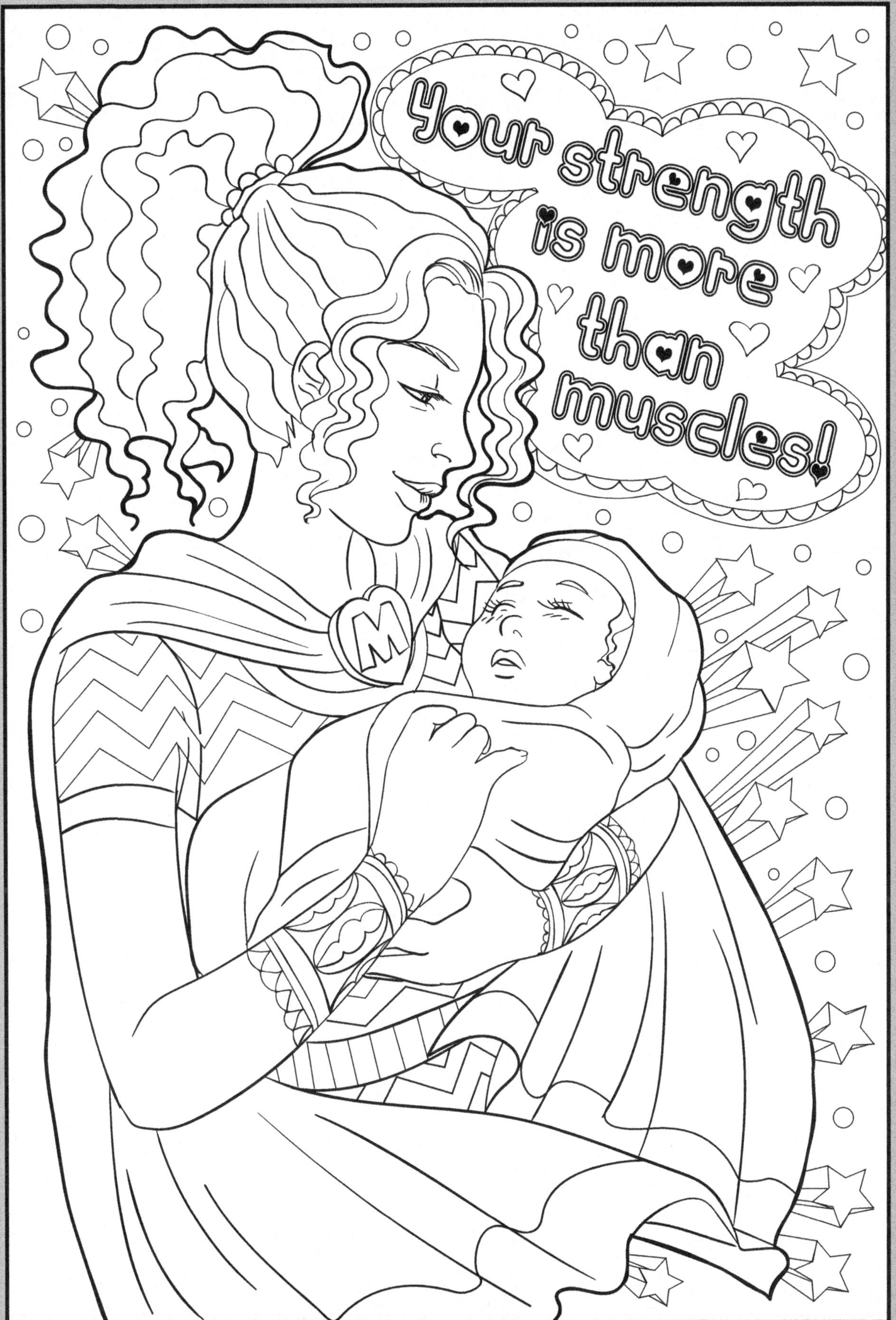
Your strength is more than muscles!
M

Today is the day, Mama! You did it! Congrats!
You have made it to the end of the journal.
Take time and reflect on your journey.

Made in the USA
Columbia, SC
19 February 2023